M000073323

S*Every*car

S*Tells a*tory

Yolanda Hawley

ISBN 978-1-64471-651-9 (Paperback)
ISBN 978-1-64471-828-5 (Hardcover)
ISBN 978-1-64471-652-6 (Digital)

Copyright © 2019 Yolanda Hawley
All rights reserved
First Edition

All rights reserved. No part of this publication may be reproduced, distributed, or transmitted in any form or by any means, including photocopying, recording, or other electronic or mechanical methods without the prior written permission of the publisher. For permission requests, solicit the publisher via the address below.

Covenant Books, Inc.
11661 Hwy 707
Murrells Inlet, SC 29576
www.covenantbooks.com

Contents

Jack William Hawley

Every Scar Tells a Story

THIS BOOK IS BASED ON true events. The reason that I have decided to share my story is that I want to give hope to the hopeless. I too was once lost and without hope. I was so lost that I was blind, but now I see.

The stories I am about to share are all true. I will share with my readers that God has a plan for your lives. The reason I was born was to share my testimony with the lost and the hopeless. I can honestly say I have walked in lost and hopeless shoes. Before I received Jesus as my Lord and Savior, I was just going through the motions. I was just trying to survive. I had no idea what love was until I received Jesus as my Lord and Savior. I learned that God so loved the world that He gave His only begotten Son, that whosoever believes in Him should not perish but have everlasting life (John 3:16, KJV). Because God loved me, I am now able to love myself and others. I began living and not just surviving. My book, *Every Scar Tells a Story*, is about hope for the hopeless.

I will start off by sharing some personal information about myself, then I will be sharing some events. Events that took place before and after I received Jesus as my Lord and Savior.

My name is Jack Hawley. I was born in Los Angeles, California. I am sixty-three years old. My mom was Stella Mae Bennett Palmer, who passed away in 1987 after an open-heart surgery when she was only fifty-six years old. My dad, Donald Eugene Hawley, passed away in 1974 after a massive heart attack at the young age of forty-eight. He died of a massive heart attack after a race in Bakersfield.

I have been married to my beautiful wife, Yolanda, for forty-three years, and we have two children. Our oldest son is forty-two. His name is Jack Hawley Jr., and he is married to Sairy, who is his second wife. He has three sons. His oldest son is Jack Hawley III. He is eighteen. Jordan who is fifteen; and Joseph, his youngest son, is three. He also has a stepson, Tony, who is ten.

Our daughter is named Angeline, and she is thirty-nine years old. She is married to Jesse Paul Walker. She has been married for nine years and has a beautiful five-year-old son named Rocky. She also has a stepson, Junah, who is sixteen.

I have a brother named Don Eugene Hawley Jr. He is sixty-four. He will be mentioned in this book quite a bit. I also have a half sister, Kathy Norton. She was my mother's firstborn. She is sixty-seven years old.

This is just my immediate family. I have many nieces and nephews too many to name.

CHAPTER 1

Dysfunctional Family

I WAS BORN INTO A very dysfunctional family. My dad was a race car driver and was a three-time national champion on motorbikes and represented the United States in Europe. He was the captain. He was one of the greatest motorcycle riders that ever lived. He was also one of the greatest race car drivers in his time.

His home track was in Gardena, California, and was called Ascot Park. He would travel with his racing team all over the world. You could say that his first love was racing. Everything else took a back seat, including his family.

My dad was always working on his race cars, or he was racing somewhere. He was never home. My mother would go to all the local races with my dad. She never traveled out of state with him.

The group that my dad traveled with was a pretty rough group. The racing guys were full of life. There was always a lot of drinking in the racing circle. The racing guys were always partying, and there were always plenty of fence hangers around. Fence hangers are women that hung around after the races were over to see who they could hook up with. Their whole agenda was to hook up with as many race car drivers as possible.

This caused many problems in my parent's marriage. Both my mom and dad were very jealous of each other.

My dad, Don, had two switches. He could be the life of the party, or he could be your worst nightmare. When he would drink, he would become very violent.

One night after the races, he came home drunk. I guess he was mad because the doors were locked, and he couldn't find the right key to open the front door.

My mother was so afraid of my dad when he was drunk because my dad would use my mom as his own personal punching bag. He would be the one out drinking and carousing; however, he would always make it as my mother's fault. It didn't matter what he did. He was never wrong in his mind.

He would come home after drinking and carousing and start a fight with my mom over trivial stuff such as locking up our house after dark. It seemed like he would blame my mom for everything that went wrong in his life. No matter what my mom did, it was never good enough for my dad.

One of my first memories of my dad coming home drunk was when I was only three years old. He had been drinking all night. He came home drunk and started pounding on the front door. I guess that night my mom didn't feel like being his punching bag, so she locked all the doors and would not let my dad in.

My mother told me and my brother to hide under the bed. We were so afraid that we did exactly what she said. Before long, my mom was under the bed with us. We were all hiding from my dad. We were all crying and praying that he would just go away.

The next thing I remember was a loud noise. It sounded like our house was coming down upon us. To our horror, my dad had actually kicked the door open. He was screaming for my mom as he went through the house looking for her. He finally spotted her hiding underneath the bed with me and my brother.

He demanded that she must come out under the bed. When she wouldn't come out, he grabbed her by her hair and pulled her out. Once he got a hold of her, he started beating her. My mom was, no joke, she was a fireplug herself and started fighting back.

My brother and I could hear our mom and dad fighting. We did not dare to come out from under the bed. The next morning when my brother and I crawled out from beneath the bed, we no longer had a front door. The only thing that remained was a pile of splinters.

My parents were like oil and water; they just did not get along. They had a love-hate relationship which caused nothing but hurt and confusion for me and my brother. We felt bad when our parents would fight. You would think that we would get used to it, but it is something you never get used to.

CHAPTER 2

First Foster Home

I WAS ONLY FIVE YEARS old when my brother, Don, and I were placed in a boys' home in Riverside, California. My older brother, Don, was named after my dad, Don Hawley Sr. Don was two years older than me. The reason Don and I were placed in a boys' home was because my mom and dad were always fighting.

My brother, Don, and I were left home alone all the time to care for ourselves. We were living in Corona, California, the first time the state stepped in and took us away from our parents and placed us in our first foster home.

When I first arrived at the boys' home, I felt very scared even though my brother and I were often left alone when we lived with my mom and dad. This time, the fear I was feeling was different. This fear was a fear of the unknown.

As a little boy, I was afraid of the dark like most kids. I had legitimate reasons for my fear. For you see, it was always at night at my home that bad things would happen, like my mom and dad fighting or waking up at night to find that my brother and I were left alone once again. Fear of not having anything to eat, fear that my dad would come home drunk, fear of my dad being in a bad mood, fear of my dad fighting with my mom or my brother. Fear was something that I knew all too well.

My brother and I were placed in a dorm with about twenty other boys aged five to fifteen. In the boys' home, my brother and I had to follow rules. We had to be in bed at a certain time every night. We had to be up early in the morning before the sun even came out.

Every morning, my brother and I would have to walk across the road to a different building in the dark and in the cold just to have breakfast. The one thing that I remember about breakfast was that they had rows and rows of tables, and on every table, there was a half of a grapefruit for each child.

I remember before we could eat breakfast, all the boys had to bow their heads and pray over their food. I remember that we prayed before we had breakfast, lunch, and before we ate dinner. We even prayed every night before we went to bed. I wasn't sure about all the praying that was going on in the boys' home, but for some reason, it did seem to help me sleep better after we would pray.

All the boys living in the home had chores. I remember after school, one of my chores was raking up all the leaves around the boys' home. I would start raking as soon as I got home from school and couldn't come in until dinnertime. We would then take our shower and get ready for bed.

It had been two weeks in the boys' home before I finally realized I wasn't going to see my parents for a while. This made me very sad. I could not understand why my mom or dad did not come and get me and my brother. I felt that no one loved us. The only thing that kept me going was knowing that my brother was with me.

While in the boys' home, I remembered two of the older boys getting into a fight. The Chaplin of the boys' home was called Papa Germany. When kids would get in trouble for fighting or doing something wrong in school, Papa Germany would grab them underneath their chins and shake them really hard.

I remember that there was a really mean lady in the boys' home. When one of the boys would get in trouble for not listening to her, she would grab them and put their heads in the toilet. She would do this as a punishment.

My brother and I promised each other that we would never let that wicked old lady put our heads in the toilet. She tried one time, but I fought back, and she never tried again. She would also grab a twig from one of the many trees around the boys' home and hit the boys on their legs when they were goofing off. So needless to say, nobody in the boys' home liked her. We all called her the Wicked Witch of the West.

I was in school for only two and a half weeks when I got in my first fight. I knew that when I got back to the boys' home that I was going to be in trouble. I was called into Papa Germany's office. Papa Germany asked me why I got in a fight. I told him because the older boy was picking on one of the younger kids. Papa Germany grabbed me from under my chin and was shaking me so hard that I thought my head was going to fall off.

He was telling me that fighting was not allowed. My punishment for getting in a fight was Papa Germany's attention getter. The grabbing of my chin and shaking me like a rag doll was just part of my punishment. The other half of my punishment included raking all the leaves and mopping all the bathroom floors. You have to remember I was only five years old at this time. I told myself that I was not going to get into any more fights. I did not want to deal with Papa Germany's anger. I was not stupid! I hated it when Papa Germany grabbed my chin. I remembered it hurt really bad. I told myself that I was going to stay out of trouble.

It was only a couple weeks later when I got into my second fight. From a young age, I was never one to back down from a fight. When I got back to the boys' home, I knew I would be in trouble. The main caregiver told me that Papa Germany was going to deal with me later for getting into another fight. That's all that I needed to hear. I told my brother what had happened. I told him I did not want to be punished again. My brother told me not to worry because he had a plan.

That night, my brother, Don, decided that we were going to run away. After dinner, me and my brother, Don, and one of his friends decided that once the lights went out and everyone was in bed, we would run away from the boys' home.

I remember being afraid, but I also knew that I did not want to deal with Papa Germany. That night after all the lights went out, we took off our pajamas and put on our street clothes. We quietly snuck out the back door, then we all started running down this dark alley.

When we got to the end of the alley, to our horror, was the police station.

Me, Don, and one of his friends ran right into the parking lot of the police station. When we got to the parking lot of the police station, a policeman turned into the parking lot spotting all of us, and he quickly got out of his police car and grabbed us.

This was the first time I had ever seen the inside of a jail, but sadly, it would not be my last. The policeman knew right away that we were from the Christian home for boys. He put us in the back of his police car and took us back to the boys' home with a warning not to run away again. And there were to be worse consequences.

When the three of us boys got back to the boys' home, we were punished. Not only did we have to do our regular chores, we had to do extra chores. It seems like all we did was go to school, come home, and do our chores. I remember that I had to use this large machine to buff the floors after they were mopped. It seemed like all I did was rake leaves and clean. This went on for over a year.

The only good thing about running away from the boys' home was that some of the older boys thought that my brother and I were cool and brave for running away.

CHAPTER 3

Jack and Don Left the Boys' Home

AFTER A YEAR IN THE boys' home, I thought I would never see my mom or dad again. I had given up all hope that I would ever see my parents. I was actually getting used to not having my parents around. I was finally getting used to all the rules in the boys' home. I was abiding by the rules and trying to stay out of trouble.

I actually liked the fact that we always had something to eat for breakfast, lunch, and dinner. This was something I never had growing up with my mom and dad. I was even getting used to all the praying even if it was just over my food and praying that God would watch over us as we slept during the night.

One day, out of the blue, my brother and I were called into Papa Germany's office. When my brother, Don, and I got to the office, we were so surprised. Sitting in Papa Germany's office was our mom.

At first, I couldn't believe my eyes. My mom was actually sitting in Papa Germany's office. I thought, *Could this really be true?* I must be dreaming.

At that point, I didn't care if I was dreaming or not. All I can remember is just running and giving my mom the biggest hug ever. I was so glad to see her. I was so glad that I wasn't dreaming.

Once I finally stopped hugging my mom, I noticed my dad was nowhere to be found. I thought to myself, *Why isn't my dad here with my mom?*

Before I could figure everything out, Papa Germany stood up from behind his big desk. He came around to where my brother and I were. He stood there looking at my brother and I for a while, then he gave us both a handshake and told us to be good boys. He told us to go to our rooms and gather up all our belongings. Then he told us we were going to be leaving the boys' home and that we were going to be living with our mother and our grandparents in Corona, California.

I remember, as I was packing up my things, I actually felt a little sad to be leaving the boys' home. I didn't know if I wanted to cry or if I wanted to jump for joy. Once again, I was afraid. I was fearful of the unknown.

CHAPTER 4

The Train Track and Conductor

WHEN MY BROTHER AND I went to live with my mom, who at that time was living with her mom and stepdad, there were no rules or chores. My brother and I did whatever we pleased.

We lived across from the train tracks. My brother and I would play in a swamp near the tracks. We also played on the train tracks. We would line up rocks, cans, or whatever we could find on the tracks, then we would watch the train flatten them out. We would pick up rocks and throw them at the train as it passed by. We did a lot of crazy things down by the tracks. We were two boys who had absolutely no structure or supervision in our lives.

One day as we were throwing rocks at the train, we accidentally hit the caboose and shattered the glass window that was about two feet tall. An hour later, we saw these two guys that actually worked on the trains coming toward me and my brother. They asked us if we knew anything about some kids throwing rocks at the train. We told them that we had seen two boys running across the swamp and that they might be the boys that they were looking for.

We told the two guys to go across the swamp where my brother and I had actually made a trap. The two guys got stuck in the mud. They were up to their knees in the mud. My brother and I started laughing at the two guys. Then my brother and I ran home as fast as we could.

A few hours later, there was a knock on the door. When my grandmother opened the door, I could see two police officers standing in the doorway. They asked my grandmother if they could talk to me and my brother. And of course, my grandmother said yes, and they asked us if we knew anything about some kids throwing rocks at the train. We told the police officers we had no idea what they were talking about. The police officers then asked my grandmother if she wouldn't mind accompanying them to the scene of the accident. They wanted to take me and my brother to meet the train conductor.

We tried talking our grandmother into not letting us go. She told us if we didn't do anything wrong, then we had nothing to worry about. She agreed to go with the police officers, so off we all went.

As soon as my brother and I saw the train conductor, we knew we were in trouble. The train conductor's forehead was covered in blood. When we threw the rock, it shattered the glass in the caboose. A piece of the glass cut the conductor's forehead.

My brother and I told the police officers that they had the wrong boys, but the train conductor told the police officer that he recognized me and my brother as being the boys who threw the rocks.

Finally, my brother and I confessed that we were the boys that had thrown the rock at the caboose of the train. We told the train conductor that we never meant to hurt him and that we were very sorry.

At that point, the police officers told my grandmother that they had to take me and my brother to the police station and that they had to make an incident report. They told my grandmother that they would not release us until our legal guardians came and got us. My grandmother finally got a hold of my mom, and when my mom got to the police station and saw that Don and I were in trouble again, she just started crying.

She asked us why we wanted to hurt her by always getting in trouble. At this point, the train conductor told the police officers that he did not want to press charges. He told me and my brother that throwing rocks at the trains was very dangerous. He told us that we should never throw rocks at a train. We assured him that we had learned our lesson and that we would not be throwing rocks ever again. At that point, my brother and I were released to go home with our mom.

CHAPTER 5

Rewarded for Getting in Trouble

AFTER MY BROTHER AND I got out of jail for throwing rocks at the train and splitting the conductors head wide open, instead of going home and being punished, my mom and grandparents took me and my brother to the bike store in downtown Corona. They took us into the bike store and told us to pick out any bike we wanted.

I remember thinking that we should be punished for throwing rocks and hurting the conductor, but instead, we were in a bike store picking out a bike. It just didn't make any sense. It was like we were being rewarded for being bad. I remember my brother picked out this really cool red bike, and I picked out a blue bike.

After my grandparents paid for the bikes, instead of trying to get them in the car, they let me and my brother ride our bikes from downtown Corona all the way home across the train tracks. It was probably a ten-mile ride from the bike store to our house.

I remember being a little confused because in the boys' home, whenever we did something wrong, we were punished. Now living with my mom and grandparents, whenever we did something wrong, it seemed like we got rewarded instead of being punished.

Looking back on it now, I think my mother felt guilty for putting us in the boys' home and was trying to make up for it by buying us stuff. I think my mom knew that she would never get voted as the best mom in town. She really had no idea how to raise me and my brother. She was just doing the same thing that her mother did when raising her.

Instead of being there physically, she just thought that she could buy her love by giving of material things. My mom was doing the same thing. She probably felt guilty that neither she or my dad were ever there for me and my brother.

When we were little and my mom and dad were still together, my mom wanted to be with my dad whenever he was racing. He was racing all the time, and my mother did not trust him because there was always women around wanting to be with my dad. Plus, my mother did not want to miss out on any of the partying that went on before and after the races. Now that my parents were divorced, my mother was trying to make it up to me and my brother for never being around and by buying our love with gifts.

Unfortunately, this did not work, and my brother and I were constantly getting in trouble. By this time, my mom started doing drugs to ease the pain that she was feeling. I think she was hurt over the divorce and that she had regrets about putting me and my brother in a home for boys.

I remember her always being loaded. We were lucky that she never burned down the house. She was a chain-smoker, and when she was loaded, the ashes from her cigarettes would fall on the floor or wherever she was sitting at the time. She would burn holes into the carpet, sofa, and her bedding. It seemed like all the blankets in our house had cigarette burns on them.

She could not take care of herself, so how in the world could she take care of me and my brother? The answer is easy—she couldn't. My mother decided that my brother and I would have to go live with our father. She just couldn't take care of me and my brother, and in all fairness, my brother and I were a handful.

CHAPTER 6

Sent to Live with My Dad

ONCE MY MOM HAD DECIDED that my brother and I were too much for her to handle, she sent us to live with our dad. By this time, I was eight, and my brother was ten. My dad lived on 119th Street in Los Angeles, California. He lived right across the street from the elementary school, the same school that my brother and I would soon attend. My dad enrolled both me and my brother into the school.

My dad was a no-nonsense-kind-of-guy. He was really strict. My brother and I had to walk a very fine line. My brother was always being beaten by my dad. For some reason, my brother was always pushing my dad's buttons. I was very afraid of my dad and tried to stay out of his way.

We had been living with our dad for about two months when I got into my first fight at school. I had beaten up the boy pretty bad, but in my defense, the boy had bit me. I was really afraid that when I got home from school my dad was going to beat me, but instead, he had to take me to the hospital, and I had to get a TB shot.

When we got home from the hospital, my dad told me he was glad that I hadn't backed down from a fight. He also told me that the next time I got in a fight, make sure that I did not fight in school. He wanted to make sure that if I got in a fight that I would make sure to fight off-campus so that I wouldn't get in trouble.

One night when my dad was out, my brother, his friend Ed, and I were bored. We decided to go outside and play. We came across a truck that had the keys in it. My brother, his friend Ed, and I decided that we were going to take the truck for a joyride.

Since Ed was the oldest, he got in the driver's seat. And I was sitting in the middle of the truck, and my brother was sitting shotgun. Ed was probably twelve and could not drive a stick shift. This, however, did not stop him from starting up the truck and driving down the street.

When we spotted a police car, Ed tried to park the truck, but instead, he hit the wrong gear and drove up and over the sidewalk. Ed ran right into a telephone pole. When the police officer turned on his lights, we all jumped out of the truck and took off running. I remember hopping a couple of fences and hiding under a bench.

When a big black Rottweiler spotted me and was trying to bite me, I was able to get away by running down the alley to our house and hiding in my dad's garage. I could hear the police officer running past the garage and could see their flashlights shining in the dark. I heard some noise outside the garage and realized that it was my brother, Don. I called to my brother, and he came into the garage. We both stayed there for a while. Then my brother told me to go upstairs.

When we got upstairs, we heard someone knocking on the door. Don told me to put my pajamas on, and he did the same thing. We were going to pretend that we were sleeping. We were scared and didn't want to answer the door. Our dad was not home, and it was late.

The person at the front door would not stop knocking. My brother, Don, thought it might be his friend Ed, so he went downstairs and opened the door. To his surprise, it was not his friend Ed, it was a police officer.

The police officer told us to get our parents. We told him that we only lived with our dad and that he wasn't home. The police officer told us to go upstairs and get dressed. He told us that we had to go with him. We told the police officer that we couldn't go with him. We told the police officer that if our dad came home and found that we were not home, we would be in trouble.

The police officers said it was too late for that, that we were already in trouble. He pointed to the back seat of his police car and said, "See that kid handcuffed in the back seat of my car? He just got busted for stealing a truck and guess what? He said that you and your younger brother were both with him and that it was your idea."

If looks could kill, my brother, Don, could have killed Ed that night. My brother and I changed out of our PJs and into our street clothes. The police officer took us back to the scene of the crime, where there were now two other police cars and four other police officers. They were talking to the guy that owned the truck.

When we got there, the police officer got us out of the back of his car. Ed was the only one in handcuffs. As my brother and I were standing beside the police car, to our horror, our dad turned the corner in his yellow 55 Nomad. All I remember was screaming, "My dad is going to kill us!"

My brother, Don, told the police officer to please take him to jail and that he did not want to go home with our dad. The police officer waved our dad over. After what seemed to be an eternity, the police officer released us to our dad. They only took Ed to jail.

When we got home, I was still crying. My dad told me to stop crying and to go upstairs and go to bed. My brother, Don, wasn't so lucky. He got it with both barrels that night. I think my dad beat him for an hour straight.

I lay in my bed fearing for my life. I just knew that as soon as my dad was done beating my brother, it would be my turn. But for some reason, my dad never did come for me.

The next day, my dad received a phone call from the police station. They told my dad that the guy that owned the truck was not going to press charges. He just wanted my dad and Ed's dad to pay for his truck to be fixed.

Soon after that ordeal, my mom and dad got back together. Maybe my dad felt that if my mom was around, she could watch over me and my brother while he was working and racing.

When I found out that my mom and dad were getting back together, I was happy. I thought to myself that finally we could be a family—one big happy family. But boy was I wrong. It wasn't even a week before my mom and dad were at each other throats. It seemed like my mother could do nothing right. My dad was always complaining that she couldn't cook or clean. He was constantly telling her that she was good for nothing and that she was a horrible wife and a terrible mother.

Once again, my parents split up. I was glad that my mom left, at least my dad couldn't beat on her anymore. This went on over and over again, year after year. My mom and dad would fight and break up. Then a few months or even a year later, they would get back together. This was just part of my childhood.

I remember my mom and dad breaking up and getting back together all the time. It was like a revolving door for them. They actually married and divorced each other three different times. Every time they would break up, my brother and I would have to choose who we were going to live with. No child should have to make that decision. No matter who I picked, I always felt sorry for the one I didn't pick to live with. I remember the last time I picked my mom over my dad. The look on my dad's face; he was so disappointed in me. The look he had on his face still haunts me to this day.

CHAPTER 7

We Moved to Inglewood

MY BROTHER AND I MOVED to Inglewood with our mom. I was ten, and my brother was twelve. By this time, my brother and I were left alone to fend for ourselves all the time. Our mom was never around, and when she was, she was either on the nod or sleeping.

One morning, my brother and I woke up, and once again, our mom wasn't home. We were really hungry. It seemed like I was always hungry all the time. There was never any food in our house. The only thing to eat that morning was a box of dry oatmeal. No milk, no sugar, just an old box of dry oatmeal.

My brother and I put some water in a pan along with the oatmeal. Then we put the pan on the stove to make the oatmeal. It didn't work! It was just a pan full of mush. We tried eating it because we were so hungry, but we couldn't. Instead, we made little round balls, and we threw them at each other. Before you knew it, we had twenty or thirty of those balls of oatmeal all over the kitchen. They were all on the ceiling in the kitchen. We really made a mess.

We thought it was pretty funny, and at that point, we did not care what our mom would do to us. It seemed like when we were bored, we always found something to keep us entertained.

It was getting late, and my mom was still not home. My brother and I noticed that there was a miniature golf place across the field. We had always wanted to go and play miniature golf, but we never had any money. My brother and I decided that we were going to wait until the miniature golf place closed, then we would break into the miniature golf place and play a round of golf.

Once the miniature golf place was closed, my brother and I broke into the facility. We were both still really hungry as we hadn't eaten anything all day. The first thing we noticed was the shelves that were filled with candy. So before we turned the lights on to play golf at the miniature golf place, we ate candy and drank sodas until our stomachs were full.

The next day, the police came knocking on our front door. They wanted to know why we broke into the golf place. We told them we didn't know what they were talking about. They finally got a hold of our mom. My mom said that she was home with us all night and that we never left her side. She lied, and my brother and I got away with playing golf and breaking into the golf course. At that time, I thought that it was pretty funny that we got away with it.

The police officer that came to our house knew that my mom was lying. He was a really nice guy. I think he felt sorry for me and my brother. He told my mother that he was the head coach for a baseball team in Inglewood. He asked my mom if my brother and I could join his team.

My mother told him she didn't have time to take us to practice or to any of the games. He assured my mother that he would pick us up for all the practices and games and that he would drop us off at home afterward.

CHAPTER 8

Joined Inglewood Baseball Team

THE POLICE SERGEANT OF THE Inglewood Police was the head coach for the baseball team. He came back over to our house. He knew my brother and I were the kind of kids he wanted to help, given the fact that we were always getting in trouble. My brother and I started playing baseball for the first time.

The police sergeant was a nice man. He tried to help me and my brother. My brother and I were really good athletes. We were both very athletic, so playing sports came easy for us. What didn't come easy was following the rules!

As much as the police sergeant wanted to help me and my brother out, it just didn't do much good. All we knew at that time was that we just wanted to fight everybody. No matter who it was, we just wanted to fight. We liked fighting. We were causing pain to someone else. We were in pain, and we wanted others to be in pain too.

At that time, our pain came from not having what the other boys had. They had parents that loved them. They had everything they needed to play baseball. They had baseball cleats, their own glove, and bats. My brother and I had nothing. We were the kids who had to borrow everything. We did not have a baseball glove or a bat. We did not have baseball cleats. Our tennis shoes were old. I remember being one of the fastest kids on the team, but without baseball cleats, it was really hard running the bases.

Our parents never came to any of our games. We never had anybody in the stands cheering for us. This was a painful time, not having our parents around to see how good we were in sports. The pain turned into anger, and I could not control the anger that was burning inside of me. The anger was consuming me.

Once the anger came to the surface, there was really nothing I could do to stop it. It was like having an out of body experience. If I got into a fight, I couldn't stop. The police sergeant in Inglewood wanted to help me and my brother, but he just couldn't. And before long, my brother and I were sent to juvenile hall.

The court system said that we were incorrigible. Once my brother and I were put into juvenile hall, one of the first things that they wanted to do was to break us up. My brother and I were put in juvenile hall with older boys. Even though I was afraid and didn't want to be apart from my brother, it didn't stop me from fighting. It seemed like all my brother and I did was fight.

When my father found out that my brother and I were in juvenile hall and that they wanted to put us into foster system, my dad finally said that enough was enough!

CHAPTER 9

School Fight

OUR DAD GOT A HOLD of us and brought us back to Gardena where he lived on Normandie and Thirty-Ninth Street. Our dad was a perfectionist. He wanted everything done his way. We had to make sure that we left everything exactly the way we found it. If we did not clean up after ourselves, there would definitely be hell to pay.

The one cool thing about living with our dad was right down the street, there was Ramona's Mexican restaurant. My brother and I always ate at Ramona's. We would always order Ramona's burritos. To this day, some fifty years later, every time I'm in Gardena, I always make sure to stop by at Ramona's and pick up a couple of burritos.

I remember starting school. And on my very first day of school, I was getting a drink of water from the drinking faucet. This older boy, who was known as the toughest kid in school, pushed me and told me that I couldn't get a drink from that faucet.

I remembered what my dad said the last time I got in a fight. He told me to make sure that I never got in a fight at school. So I looked at the guy and told him to meet me at the big oak tree off-campus the following day. When I got home from school, I told my dad what happened. He told me that he was glad that I didn't fight the kid at school. He told me that he would be at the big oak tree the next day.

The following day, it seemed like everyone in the whole school knew that I was going to be fighting the toughest guy in school. I remember my brother, Don, telling me that this guy was really tough and that I shouldn't fight him, but it was too late for that, and I wasn't about to back down.

That day after school, I headed to the big oak tree. It seemed like half the kids from school were following me. Once I got to the oak tree, the other guy was already there with a whole bunch of his friends. I heard this loud whistle. It was what my dad called the Hawley whistle. Once I heard that whistle, I was to stop whatever I was doing and find my dad no matter where I was or what I was doing. I knew my dad was looking for me.

As I was looking in the crowd to see where the whistle was coming from, I spotted my dad standing on top of the hood of his silver 64 Thunderbird. He shouted, "Kick his ass son" and gave me the thumbs-down sign. This meant to show him no mercy. Much like in the Roman days when the emperor would tell the gladiators to kill his opponent, he would give him the thumbs-down sign. The kids were all yelling for the bully to beat up the new kid. I got on top of the guy and just start beating the crap out of him.

Once I started winning the fight, all the kids turned and started cheering for me. I beat the guy until he called "uncle." He wanted nothing to do with me.

The next day at school, I was the king of the hill. No one wanted to mess with me. My dad and my brother told me that they were proud of me. I finished out the school year without one more fight.

The following are just a couple more of my true stories that happened in my life and that once you read them, you will be scratching your head in disbelief.

CHAPTER 10

Went through the Living Room Window

THIS INCIDENT HAPPENED WHEN I was about fifteen. My brother, Don, was always picking on me. One day, my brother and I got in an argument. On this particular day, I just couldn't take it, and I lost my mind. I got so mad at my brother that I actually picked him up and ran him through the living room window of my dad's house. We both ended up out on the front lawn. I thought I'd killed him.

Once I realized what I had done, I knew that both my brother and I were in deep trouble. But at the time, I was so mad that I don't think I even cared until my dad got home and saw that the front window in our living room was shattered. Don and I knew that once our dad saw the condition of the house, we were as good as dead.

The house looked like a cyclone hit it. We were both so scared that we ran all the way to our mom's house. Our dad was so mad that he told our mother to come and pick up our belongings and that he did not want to see us because if he did, he was going to kill us. I think a year went by before my brother and I saw our dad again.

As I look back on that incident, I feel very fortunate that nothing serious had happened to me or to my brother.

After that incident, my brother and I both decided that we would never fight each other again. We both realized that one of us could get seriously hurt, and to this day, my brother and I have never gotten into a physical fight.

Jack Hawley - Age 15

CHAPTER 11

Yellow Basket

THIS INCIDENT HAPPENED WHEN I was sixteen. A couple of my friends and I went to Yellow Basket, a hamburger place in Gardena. As we went in to order our hamburgers, three people walked in—two guys and a girl. My friend Larry said something to the girl. One of the guys said something back to Larry, and a fight almost broke out right inside the Yellow Basket.

Ted, the owner of the Yellow Basket, told us to take our business outside, so those three people left, and Ted let us order our hamburgers. But after we got our food, Ted told us to eat our burgers outside. We went out and got into our truck. The truck was parked in the back parking lot of Yellow Basket. We had just pulled out our hamburgers and started eating when we looked up and noticed that the same three people that were in Yellow Basket earlier had just showed up with two cars loaded with full of people.

The first guy that got out of the car was the guy that Larry had words with. He jumped out of the truck! I was looking for something under the truck's seat—a bat, crowbar, anything. I knew I needed something! There was ten of them and only two of us. Lucky for me, there was a crowbar under the front seat of the truck. I came out of the truck and made all the other people back off.

Larry and the other guy started fighting. I was looking at the other people to make sure that they did not jump in. When I turned around to see what was going on, I saw Larry was on the ground. At first I thought he just got knocked out, but then I noticed that the guy he was fighting had a knife. I then put two and two together. Larry had just been stabbed with a knife. When I reached down to help him, I noticed that there was blood everywhere. I seriously thought at that time that he was dead.

All of the other guys took off running. They all ran down across the street to the gas station. I caught up to the guy that stabbed him. I hit him across his head and shoulders with the crowbar and knocked him out. I then turned around and was after a couple more guys. I was fighting for my life at that point. By that time, someone had called the police and an ambulance.

One of the police officers tackled me to the ground. I had rolled over on top of him and was punching him until I knocked him out. I did not realize that he was a police officer until the other police officer kicked me in the head. Once I got on my feet, I realized that I had knocked out a police officer. By that time, it seemed like there were three or four other cops' cars that just showed up. They were all over me trying to take me to the ground.

When I was on the ground, they all started hitting me with billy clubs. I got hit several times on my forehead. They finally knocked me out. When I finally came to, I had a knot on my forehead that was the size of a baseball. They took me to the police station.

There were two different ambulances, one that took Larry to the hospital and the other took the guy that had stabbed Larry to Harbor General Hospital. Once I was in the police station, I explained what had happened. I told them that I did not mean to hit the police officer, that I was just trying to stick up for my friend. The police officer called my mother to come and pick me up at the police station.

When my mother got to the police station and saw what the police officers had done to my forehead, I thought she was going to lose her mind. She must have called those police officers every name in the book. They couldn't get us out of the police station fast enough.

We found out which hospital they took Larry to, and we went to the hospital to see how he was doing. They had to operate him. They literally filleted him like a fish. Luckily for him, he made it through the surgery.

I remember my mother and I stayed at the hospital all through the night just to make sure that he was going to be okay. Thank God, he made it. To this day, he has a scar that starts from the top of his chest that runs down pass his belly button. His family did press charges against the guy that stabbed him, and of course, they won their case in court. Whether or not they received any money for damages, I don't know. We really didn't talk about it.

The guy that I hit with the crowbar tried to take me to court as well. I claimed self-defense, and everything was thrown out of court. To this day, I'm not sure if the guy that stabbed Larry ever got any jail time. He's lucky that he didn't die, or he would still be in jail for murder.

CHAPTER 12

First Trip to the Snow

ONE WEEKEND, MY BROTHER, DON, and our friend Steve decided we all wanted to go to the mountains. We barely had enough money for gas to get us up and down the mountain. We didn't have any snow clothes or ski equipment. But once we put our minds to doing something, we would find a way to do it.

My brother and Steve decided to stop at a store where they rented ski equipment. I went into the store like I owned it. I tried on a snow jumpsuit. The best one they had in the store was like $300. I got the matching jacket which was another $300. I literally put on everything you would need to go to the snow. From the top of my head to the bottom of my feet. I had all the bells and whistles. I had the best of everything. I also got the best skis that they had in the store.

When I was done getting everything I needed for the snow, it probably totaled over $2,000. I didn't even have $10 in my pocket. I just walked out of the store like I owned the place.

There was a guy that came out of the store that worked there. He came up to me and said, "Hey, you can't steal that stuff."

He told me to bring everything back in, and if I didn't, he was going to call the police. I told him I was going to beat him up really bad before the police could even reach the store. I suggested to him that he mind his own business. I told him to get away from us or that I was going to put him in the hospital. He just turned and walked away. He didn't want any problems.

I then told Steve to head up to the mountains. My brother and Steve couldn't believe what I had just done. They were both laughing so loudly as we drove away. When they finally stopped laughing, they both looked at me at the same time and asked me why I didn't get them an outfit. We all started laughing again.

The funny thing was that I've never been to the mountains. I knew nothing about snow skiing. I was always doing this kind of stuff because I never had any money. I just stole what I wanted, hoping someone would say something.

Once we got to the mountains, we didn't have any money for food, so I basically did the same thing that I did at the ski shop. I walked into the grocery store, got a grocery cart, and filled it up with all kinds of groceries, from steaks to cold beers. Once the cart was filled, I just walked out of the store and told my brother to open the trunk of the car. I literally picked up the whole grocery cart and dumped the cart in the trunk with all the food, and we just took off.

Once we finally got to the mountains, I hopped on one of the lifts. As I looked down, I saw my buddy Steve coming down the slope so fast, and he had three snow patrol guys chasing him. It looked like the Keystone cops. It had to be one of the funniest things I had ever seen. The reason that they were chasing Steve was because he had stolen a pair of skis. I thought for sure he was going to go to jail that day.

To my surprise, Steve got away with it. My brother and I were sitting in one of the restaurants by the fireplace, and lo and behold, Steve walks in the joint. He said he just hid in some trees. Steve said it was like he was 007 trying to get away from the three snow patrol guys that were chasing him.

He looked at me and my brother. "I guess I just got away with that one," he said. We all just started laughing. We couldn't believe what we all got away with that day. I think we were always looking for trouble, and sometimes we would find it. I really don't know how we got away with all of the crazy things we did.

CHAPTER 13

Jack in the Box

THIS IS ANOTHER INCIDENT THAT happened with me and my friend Rick. We were both about sixteen years old. We were at Jack in the Box in Gardena. It was on Crenshaw Boulevard across the street from El Camino College.

We had ordered a hamburger. And when we left Jack in the Box, Rick had said something to one of the guys in the restaurant. By the time we got back to our car, the guy that Rick said something to had run and told several of his buddies that we're in a van in the parking lot of Jack in the Box.

To this day, I still don't know what Rick said to them, but whatever he said, it must have been something bad because before we knew what was going on, we were surrounded by six guys. Even though it was Rick that said something, I was the one that always had to get us out of trouble. I asked them if I could fight them one at a time.

They said okay, so I squared off with the first guy and knocked him out. I got to the second guy and beat him up. When I got to the third guy, they all said, "We're good." They said they were cool with everything, and they all left.

The funny thing was that Rick never stepped in to help me fight any of the guys. I looked over at Rick, and he was like a cheerleader. He was on a brick wall cheering me on. Seriously, that guy was always starting fights. He just never finished what he started.

CHAPTER 14

Bar Fight

THIS STORY HAPPENED WHEN I was eighteen. I was with my buddy Rick. This was just one of many incidents that happened with Rick and his big mouth.

Rick was one of those guys that when he got drunk, he had a habit of running his mouth. His mouth was always getting him in trouble. He never knew when to shut up. There were a least two or three different incidents that I was with Rick that his big mouth got us into trouble.

This incident almost cost Rick his life. Rick was always looking for a fight, and on this particular night, Rick found the fight he was looking for. His mouth got us into trouble again. We were at a bar on Hawthorne Boulevard. Even though I was only eighteen, we never got carded at this bar.

Rick and I just stopped in for a couple of beers. We decided to shoot a game of pool. I was standing at the pool table when I heard Rick tell some guy at the bar to shut up. The guy was yelling at his old lady. Rick told the guy that he was too loud. The guy told Rick to shut up, or he was going to kick his ass.

When he said that, Rick started walking toward the guy. The guy pulled out his knife and stuck Rick with it. Rick did not have a chance. He never knew what hit him. It all happened so fast. Rick went down and was bleeding everywhere. I ran over to him. I knew Rick was hurt really bad.

He looked up at me. "That dirty sucker stabbed me," he said. "Take me to the hospital! I don't want to die!"

I picked him up and lay him on the back seat of his car. I did this to keep him safe. I saw that there was a garage door open next to the bar. I ran in the garage and on the side of the garage, I found a rake. I broke the rake in half, then I ran back into the bar. I went after the guy that had stabbed Rick.

He was trying to get his hand in his pocket. He was trying to pull out his knife again. I hit him in the forehead before he had a chance to pull out his knife. I hit him so hard with the rake that I completely knocked him out. I hit him again and again. I was so mad. I beat him up pretty good. I thought that I had killed him.

Rick saw that I had run into the garage. He then went into the garage after me and found a red devil window scraper. I will never forget what Rick did to that guy next. He hit that guy in the face with that window scraper several times.

By the time Rick and I got done with the guy, his face looked like something you would see in a horror movie. I don't remember what happened next. All I do remember was thinking this guy was dead. I told Rick we had to get out of the bar. We had to get out before the police came.

We left and I should've taken Rick to the hospital. But I didn't. We both thought if we went to the hospital, we would be arrested for murder. Instead, we just went back to my house. Rick and I had passed out.

Lucky for us, my mom came home a couple hours later. She took one look at Rick and knew that he was in trouble. She immediately called the ambulance. They came and picked Rick up. The paramedics tried to stop the bleeding before they took Rick to the hospital.

Once the paramedics got to the hospital, the doctors took Rick straight into the operating room. They operated him all night to save his life. Later on that night at the hospital, my mom was so mad at me. She couldn't believe that Rick had almost died.

The doctors told us that Rick would've died if we hadn't brought him to the hospital when we did. The guy in the bar was also in the same hospital. The police asked both Rick and the guy in the bar what had happened. They both told the police their side of the story. They guy that stabbed Rick got in trouble for attempted murder. Rick almost died that night, and I almost lost one of my friends. It was only by the grace of God that Rick is still alive today.

CHAPTER 15

Bowling Alley

THIS IS ANOTHER INCIDENT THAT also happened when I was with Rick. Rick and his big mouth. We were leaving the bowling alley in Gardena one night when Rick reached over and touched some lady on her butt. She must have told her husband what Rick did to her because as we were walking out of the front door of the bowling alley, this guy drove his car right in front of where we were coming out.

He got out of his car then walked straight up to where we were standing. "Which one of you little punks touched my wife?"

I looked over at Rick waiting for him to say something. When I did, this guy, out of the blue, punched me so hard that he literally broke my jaw. I went down to the ground. My brother was there, and he started to fight the guy. I told my brother to stop! I told him to not touch him, that this was now my fight. I was so mad that the guy hit me when I was not even looking. I told my brother that I wanted to fight him.

When I got up, the guy and I started fighting. He was actually getting the best of me when I finally got underneath him and picked him up and drove his head straight into the ground. His head was in between his car tire and the curb. It was wedged in between so that he couldn't move. I hit him four or five times and knocked him out. I beat him up pretty good.

Rick was the one that started it by touching the guy's wife's butt. Rick should have gotten his butt kicked that night. He was always doing dumb stuff. But once again, I was the one that had to finish what Rick started.

We called Rick the cheerleader because he was the one on the sidelines cheering instead of fighting.

Someone in the bowling alley called the police. I went into the bowling alley to wash my hands and my face. And when I walked out with my brother, Don, and Rick, the police were outside waiting for us.

They asked the guy from the bowling alley which one of us was the guy that he had gotten into a fight with. He took a long look at us, then he told the police officers, "It was none of these guys. The guy I fought with was much bigger than any of these guys."

The police let us go. As we were walking away, I happened to looked back. The guy that I had fought looked at me and then gave me the thumbs up. I had just whipped his butt, and he gave me respect. I have to say he was one of the toughest guys that I ever got into a fight with. He actually broke my jaw. I guess it is easy to break someone's jaw if the person happens to be looking in the opposite direction. Needless to say, I was drinking out of a straw for months after that fight.

CHAPTER 16

Denny's Restaurant

IN THIS STORY, I WAS with my brother, Don, and my friend Joe. I called him Joe Mama. We were all stoned from smoking weed, and we were all hungry. We all wanted to stop and eat at Denny's. The only problem was that none of us had any money.

When we stopped, we knew we didn't have any money between us; however, after smoking some weed, we were all starving. We decided that we were going to eat and run. We would do this all the time. We would order our food, and once we were finished eating, we would make our way to the bathroom. Then we would just sneak out without paying.

Once we were in Denny's, we ordered everything on the menu—from their chicken fried steak to the New York steak. We ordered mashed potatoes and gravy. We ordered everything you could think of. We did not hold back. We ordered all the trimmings. We even ordered apple pie for dessert.

The waitress must have known something was up as we were ordering way too much food. It was so funny; we were laughing our guts off.

I looked up from the table, and I noticed both Don and Joe had bolted for the restroom. And I found myself just sitting there alone. Both Don and Joe had walked straight outside after going to the restroom.

I noticed that our waitress was talking on the phone and thought it would be a perfect time to make my way out of the restaurant. I got up and made my way to the bathroom. When I came out, I saw that there was a cop standing outside the front door of Denny's. I told myself that I was just going to run past the police officer. I was always a really fast runner.

Our car was parked in the back of Denny's parking lot. As I started to run out of the restaurant, the police officer was waiting for me. He went to grab me. And when he did, I punched him. I hit him so hard that it literally turned him around. I then threw him into some bushes outside of Denny's. I started running as fast as I could.

I ran around the back to where our car was parked. The police officer that I hit got up from the bushes. He was so mad that he took a shot at me with his gun. He actually hit the car door. Lucky for me, the back car window was open. I jumped into the car by the way of the open window. Joe Mama took off as the cop was shooting at us. We hopped on the freeway as we drove up around the ramp.

We looked down at Denny's, and there were three other cops' cars assembled there. We hurried and got off on the next off-ramp. Once again, we got away from the police.

The next day, we read about it in the morning paper. We thought it was funny because we didn't get caught. As I look back on it, I don't think it was funny at all. I could've been killed or my brother, and Joe Mama could've been killed. It was a miracle that no one got hurt. I believe God has always had His hand on my life even back then. I know now that God had a plan for me and my brother, Don.

Today, my brother, Don, is a pastor in San Pedro, California. He has his own church. As for me, I share my testimony every chance I get. God has changed my life.

CHAPTER 17

Stealing Meat from a Warehouse

I HAVE A MILLION STORIES of what has happened to me before I was saved. I am just going to share a couple more then I will get to the good stuff, which is when I received Jesus as my Lord and Savior. I stopped doing crazy things, and I started living my life for Jesus.

One night, my buddy Joe Mama and I were driving around looking for something to do. Joe said that he knew where we could get some steaks and some ham.

"Let's go!" I said.

We drove from Vermont in Gardena all the way down to Redondo Beach Boulevard. There were trains and a lot of warehouse buildings in that area. We went in through a window of one of the warehouses. There were boxes and boxes of dairy products.

In the back of the warehouse was the frozen area where there had to be at least a thousand steaks in boxes. It was incredible! We put this great big stack of steaks together. Then we hooked the steaks on this long pole.

If you can imagine, the pole was thirty feet long. Joe was at one end, and I was at the other end. The steaks were bouncing in the middle. We finally made our way out the window. We were going across the railroad tracks when Joe fell in the mud.

It was pretty funny. He was trying to keep the steaks from the mud. We were out there laughing our brains off. It was so funny. We ended up selling all the meat.

We went back the following night to do it again, but this time, we took one more of our friends with us. Only this time, the police were hiding in the boxes inside the warehouse. They jumped out of the boxes to get to us. Our friend got caught, but Joe and I got away. Our friend got probation, yet nothing happened to me and Joe.

Chili Bowl 2015 Midget Nationals

Brother Don, Sister Kathy, and Jack Senior 2018

CHAPTER 18

Stealing Beer from a Dairy

HERE IS ONE MORE OF my crazy stories. One night, we were going to a party. When we got there, they had just run out of beer, so I told them I would be right back with some more beer. We went to one of those dairy where you drive up and get a gallon of milk, but it was closed. So we went in the back of the building and broke into it. We opened the door, and we got several cases of beer. We must have had at least fifty cases of beer. We put the beer in the back of our van. We took all of the candy as well.

We went back to the party, dropped off the cases of beer, and went back for more. When we got there, there was a police car, and they had three or four guys with their hands up against the wall. These guys got busted for what we did. They had seen what we had done. And when we left, they went in and tried to do the same thing. Only they got caught. Once again, I got away with yet another one.

CHAPTER 19

Going through the Windshield with Brian

THIS IS ONE OF THE times that I didn't get away with one. I have the scars on my face to remind me every day that you should not ever drink or take any kind of drugs while you are behind the wheel.

I was driving around with my friend Brian. Brian was behind the wheel, and I was sitting shotgun. We were coming or going somewhere. I really don't remember as I was too loaded to remember anything. What I do remember was actually waking up in the hospital.

Brian had hit a parked car going about 40 mph. It felt like he was going 100 mph. We were both so loaded at the time that no one really knows how fast or slow we were going. Brian was lucky nothing happened to him. I think the steering wheel saved him.

I wasn't so lucky. I actually went through the windshield of the car. I was so out of it that when I went through the windshield, instead of waiting for someone to help me, I actually pulled my face back out of the windshield, leaving half of my face on the broken windshield glass.

I almost cut my eyebrow completely off along with my eyelid. I almost lost my right eye completely. I cut off the tip of my nose along with having a large cut on my right cheek. The doctors worked on me for a couple of hours. I had over three hundred stitches in my face.

The road to recovery was long and hard. I had to see a plastic surgeon several times just to get the glass that was embedded in my face out. I had to have more shots in my face and around my eye, then I care to remember, they were so painful. It was a long process on trying to heal both physically and mentally.

My sweet Yolanda was by my side. She never left my side. She has always stood by me right or wrong. She was someone I could always count on. She took care of me, loving me every step of the way. She helped me get back to square one again. No matter what I did, my sweet Yolanda was always by my side.

I know for a fact that my Heavenly Father has always been by my side. He has always protected me even when I made the wrong choices. The scars on my face are just a reminder that there are consequences for your sins.

My friends used to call me Fabian. After the accident, some of them started calling me Mussy. It has been over forty years since that horrible accident.

Forty years later, I still have the scars to remind me that I could have lost my life that night. Once again, I knew God was watching over me. God has always been with me. In His word "the Bible," God says He will never leave us or forsake us. We are the ones that leave and forsake Him. He's always right by our side.

I'm sure you seen the picture of the two sets of footprints in the sand. Then it turns into one set of footprints. The story goes as the young man was walking he looked behind, and he noticed that there was only one set of footprints in the sand. He cried out to God and asked Him, "Why when I needed you the most, you left me."

God replied, "I never left you, my son. The one set of footprints you see in the sand are mine. The reason your footprints are not in the sand is because I was carrying you in your time of trouble."

Looking back at the footprints in the sand, I know that my God has carried me time and time again. God has carried me, and He will carry you too. It is what He does. God loves us! He has the scars on His hands, on His feet, and on His side to prove it.

CHAPTER 20

Going through the Windshield with Joe Mama

THIS IS ANOTHER INCIDENT THAT happened when I was with my friend Joe Mama. We had spent the evening at Ascot Park watching the races and drinking. After the races, all I remember was getting in the car with Joe Mama. The parking lot was packed full of cars. There had to be at least a thousand cars in the parking lot.

Joe made his way out of the parking lot. And all I remember was that when I woke up, there was no longer any cars in the parking lot. Joe and I were both laid out on the front of Joe's hood of his car. We were at a stop sign. I guess Joe hit the car in front of him.

We will never know what really happened because we were both so loaded. All I remember was when we woke up, we were the only car around. Once again, Joe and I could've been seriously hurt, but we both walked away with just a few cuts and bruises. I had stitches on my face, and Joe had stitches on his inner leg where he had cut himself pretty bad.

I cannot even count how many times things like this happened. I would wake up and look out my window just to see if my car was there because I couldn't remember how I got home.

CHAPTER 21

River Trip

ONE OF MY FAVORITE PLACES on earth is the Colorado River. I have been going to the Colorado River for over forty-five years. The story that I am about to share happened when I was in my early twenties.

One weekend, I decided to go to the river with seven of my good buddies. We were staying at Red Rock Campground in Parker, Arizona. Red Rock was right next door to Fox's, a well-known place at the river, a place where everyone hangs out.

Fox's had a floating bar, the kind where you can drive your boat right up to the bar. To get to Fox's from Red Rock is within walking distance. As soon as my buddies and I got settled in at our campsite, we decided to walk over to Fox's. We were all drinking and having a good time.

After a while, five of us decided to walk back to our campsite, and we had to walk pass this campsite where a biker club had set up camp. Two of our friends decided to stay at Fox's and drink a little longer.

An hour went by, and one of the guys that was with us came running back to our campsite. He told us that our friend Mike had just gotten beaten up badly and that it was done by members of the biker club. There were about twenty bikers with their motorcycles.

I guess they did not like us walking through their campsite. They were partying just like us. Mike had said something to one of their guys, and I guess he did not take too kindly to the remark. And before Mike even knew what was going, some of the guys in the biker club just started beating him up.

My buddy Brian said, "Let's go over there. They can't get away with beating up one of our friends!"

I told him that he was crazy and that we are not going over there as I'd rather not die tonight. There was twenty of them and only seven of us. All of the guys in our group said that they were not going to go with Brian.

Brian said that he was going over there with or without us. My brother and I finally agreed to go with Brian because we did not want him to go by himself. So off the three of us went as we were all half squashed at that point.

When we got there, Brian walked right past everyone and walked into the biker's trailer. He walked into the kitchen of the trailer and got a knife. He then grabbed one of the guys by the hair and stuck the knife right in his neck. He walked him outside with the guy begging to let him go.

Brian was like a madman and said, "Okay, let's get something straight tonight. We are going to be here for the next couple of days. And when we walk by your campsite, if one more guy in our group gets hurt, I am going to come back and stick this knife in one of your necks. I would like everybody to understand that we are not here to get beaten up. We are here to have a good time! Now do we have a crystal-clear understanding of one another?"

I basically saw my life pass right before my eyes as I just could not believe what Brian was doing. It was like I was in a movie as this could not really be happening. My brother and I were looking at each other like, *Man, Brian is one crazy individual!* Even though there were twenty of them and only three of us.

The main guy told Brian, "You are one crazy dude." He then assured us that there would not be any more problems and that they would leave our guys alone. So with that, Brian put down the knife. We all started laughing like nothing had happened. And as we started to head back to our campsite, my brother, Don, and I just shook our heads in disbelief. We just could not believe what had just happened and that we were still standing.

No longer after that incident, my brother Don, Brian, and I decided that we were going to go to one of the local bars in town. The night was still young, and we wanted to go shoot a couple of games of pool.

When we walked into the bar, my buddy Brian had on a ski shirt that said "O'Brien" on the front of it. One of the guys shooting pool looked at Brian and said in a sarcastic way, "O-brain." That's all that it took, and before I even knew what was happening, Brian had grabbed a pool stick and had hit the guy over the head with it.

The guy was completely knocked out. We all left and went back to our campsite. Before we knew it, a police car drove down to where we had set up camp. Brian, Don, and I were standing in front of our campsite as the car drove down the ramp.

In the back seat of the police car was the guy that Brian had just beaten up. The police officer asked the guy if we were the guys that had knocked him out. He said yes, that we were, indeed, the guys.

Even though Don and I did not have anything to do with the altercation, the guy told the police officer that all three of us had attacked him. And with that, the police officer handcuffed the three of us and took us to jail. That had to be one of the worst nights that I have ever spent in jail. What a nightmare as I only had my trunks on, and I was not even wearing a T-shirt. I was freezing in our jail cell. In fact, we were all freezing.

I remember we all had gathered together, and were just trying to keep each other warm. My buddy Brian actually shared his T-shirt with me. If you could picture two big guys in one T-shirt, I'm sure that it had to look pretty funny. All three of us had to appear in front of the judge the following day.

She looked at us and asked why the guys from California had to come to her town and pick fights with the local guys. We all shared our story with her.

And afterward, she looked at us and said that she had our names and that she was going to let us go but that we had better not get in any more trouble or that she would put us in jail just to teach us a lesson.

As I look back on that river trip, I can see how God had protected me. A lot of my buddies were not so fortunate. My buddy Brian was murdered a few years later after our river trip. A gang member shot him in an alley in Los Angeles.

My buddy Billy was murdered in Lancaster. The police found Billy's body half buried in the Lancaster hillside. He had been shot to death over a dope deal that went wrong.

Three of my other good buddies died in motorbike accidents. Drinking and riding motorbikes just do not mix. I didn't get a chance to share the love of Jesus with my buddies, which to this day, is one of my greatest regrets. I realize now how short life really is, and I do not take one day for granted. Every day is a gift from God.

Jack, Sr. 2018

Jack, Jr. 2018

Our daughter Angeline's Family - Husband Jesse, Son's Junah and Rocky

Grandsons - Left to Right - Tony, Junah, Jordan, and Jack

CHAPTER 22

Ascot Park

HERE IS A DIFFERENT STORY that happened when I was probably around the age of seventeen. It was a Saturday night, and my brother, Don, and I had gone to the races. My dad raced almost every Saturday night at Ascot Park in Gardena, California.

On this particular night, my dad's race car broke, so my dad, my brother, and I all decided to go sit in the stands to watch the races and drink beer. I went to the concession stand to get more beer, and I noticed the line was really long. I ran up and beat this guy that was getting in the same line as I was. I said to him, "I got you!"

By the time we got up to the front of the line, he has tapped me on my shoulder and said, "No, you didn't get me! I believe that I got you!"

I looked down at his hand and saw that he had pulled out a knife. I said, "You're right, you got me. Go ahead." I waved him on so that he could pass and get in front of me. I told him that I didn't want any problems.

He was pretty stupid because as soon as he had turned around to place his order, I was lying in wait to get him. As soon as they placed his beer on the counter, I reached around and grabbed his beer and threw it in his face.

He grabbed his face because the beer was in his eyes. I hit him and knocked him to the ground. My dad and brother had seen what was going on, and once again, my dad gave me the thumbs-down sign, again, which is meant to show this guy no mercy! I don't think this guy will be pulling his knife on anybody in the near future.

The races were a place that you could get into a fight no matter what. It seems like drinking and fighting just went hand in hand.

There was another time we were at the races. It was halftime, and we were at the motorcycle races in Costa Mesa when we walked into the bathroom, and there had to be at least twenty-five or thirty guys waiting to use the bathroom.

My brother shouted out loud, "Who is the baddest person in this restroom? I want to know who you are."

It was pretty funny because everybody in the restroom said, "I am."

Sure enough, a fight broke out inside the restroom. Everybody was swinging, and guys were getting punched left and right. I couldn't believe it. We were all fighting, and it was actually kind of funny. Before we knew it, we were all outside fighting.

The police came and threw us all out of the races. This type of stuff happens all the time at the races. The races were a place where you could drink all you want. And where there's drinking, there is usually a fight that goes along with it.

Don Hawley, Sr.

CHAPTER 23

Airport Parking Lot

IT SEEMED AS IF MY dad was racing every weekend. Most of my dad's sprint car races were held at Ascot Park in Gardena, California, on Saturday nights. He would also travel to nearby races in San Diego, Bakersfield, Irwindale, and Arizona.

He had a race in San Diego one weekend, and he had called me to pick him up at the Los Angeles airport. He had been drinking and did not want to drive home drunk. I told him that it would not be a problem and that I would be there to pick him up. I had my brother, Don, to drop me off at the airport.

My dad's 1963 silver Thunderbird was parked in the airport parking lot structure. We picked up his luggage and then went to where his car was parked. My dad was on a bender and had been drinking a lot that day. When we finally got to my dad's car, I was planning on driving because my dad was drunk. I asked my dad for his keys, and he looked at me with that look that only he could give and told me that he was going to drive.

He had gotten me out of bed to drive from Gardena to LAX at 2:00 a.m., then he did not even want me to drive? *Wow!* I was a little upset, to say the least, but I was not about to argue with my dad.

I jumped in the passenger seat, and my dad jumped in behind the wheel. He drove down the ramp to the ticket booth. The guy in the booth asked my dad for his ticket. My dad was so drunk that he had forgotten where he had put the ticket. He was going through his console looking for the ticket.

The attendant could tell my dad was drunk. My dad was laughing, but the ticket attendant did not find it funny. The attendant got tired of waiting and raised his voice and told my dad that he was taking too long.

My dad looked at him and said in a stern voice, "Hold on just one minute. I'll find it. I know it is here somewhere."

The attendant then told my dad that he was taking too long and that every other car in line could not continue waiting while he attempted to find his ticket.

I thought to myself, *Oh no, this guy should not have said that*, as now my dad was really pissed off and was taking his sweet time on purpose with the intent of further upsetting the attendant, which was obviously working.

The attendant then said to my dad, "You are a f——ing idiot! Find your ticket."

My dad told the attendant that he could not find the ticket and that he needed to pull off to the side so that he could look for it.

The attendant then told him to go ahead and pull off to the side.

My dad looked at me with that silly smile and nodded his head. Oh boy, I knew then that something bad was about to happen. My dad told me to stay in the car and that he would be right back.

At that point, there was no reasoning with my dad. I did what I was told and stayed in the car. I looked back to see what my dad was going to do, but all I saw was the attendant raised about two feet in the air. My dad had grabbed the ticket attendant and had pulled him out of the little ticket booth.

He was beating the crap out of him when I saw two other guys running across the parking lot. They were going to try and help the ticket attendant that was getting beaten up by my dad. When they ran up to my dad, I got out of the car. I was going to help my dad, but my dad did not need any help.

He had grabbed the second guy and had taken him to the ground and had knocked him out. The third guy, after seeing what my dad had done to the first two guys, just took off running. He did not want anything to do with my dad.

My dad looked at me and told me, "Let's go!"

We both got back in the car with my dad in the driver's seat. He put the car in drive and took off. He then looked over at me and said, "I told the guy that I couldn't find my ticket!"

We both started laughing and thought that it was really funny.

The next day, the police called my dad and told him that he had to come down to the police station as the two ticket attendants were pressing charges against my dad for beating them up.

My dad had to hire an attorney. Lucky for him, he had a good attorney, or he could have done jail time. Instead, he just had to go to anger management classes, and I think he had to pay a couple thousand dollars in damages plus attorney fees. That airport parking ticket ended up costing my dad thousands of dollars all because my dad felt that he was being disrespected.

CHAPTER 24

Sprint Car Crash

THE RACES PLAYED A BIG part in my teenage life. My dad was one of the greatest racers that had ever lived. I enjoyed watching him race. He was one of those guys that could start in the back and still win the race.

My dad got into a really bad crash. He was running his sprint car in San Diego. The crash was so bad that my dad was knocked out. He was taken to the hospital immediately after the crash. In the hospital, he was unconscious for a week. He had hurt his arm really bad, and he could not move it. His arm was slightly paralyzed.

During this time, I noticed my brother started going to church. He was always talking to me about Jesus. I was glad that my brother had found Jesus. It was good for him. I really didn't want to have anything to do with Jesus at that point in my life.

After my dad's horrible car accident, my brother Don started talking to my dad about Jesus. My brother was always praying for me and my dad. Once my dad came home from the hospital, my brother, Don, invited our dad to his church.

The pastor gave an altar call. He asked if anyone wanted to receive Jesus as their Lord and Savior and to come forward so that he could pray for them. My dad went forward and received Jesus as his savior. I was glad that both my dad and my brother were saved. They both seemed to be at peace. This was something that I wasn't sure about.

Once my dad got saved, he started talking to me about Jesus. Now I had both my brother and my dad sharing Jesus with me. I remember after my dad got saved, he called both me and my brother at about three o'clock in the morning. He wanted us to come to his house. I could tell in his voice that he was really upset.

When we got to his house, he was sitting on the couch. He was as white as snow. He looked so afraid. I never seen my dad afraid before, so of course, I was afraid for him. He told us as he was sleeping on his couch, a beam of light hit him in his forearm right where he was injured. He said that his arm started getting really hot. He said it felt like his arm was going to fall off.

Soon after that, my dad started getting the use of his arm back. He started crying and asking God to help him and the beam of light stopped. All of a sudden, his arm was healed. He could squeeze a ball again. He had full use of his arm. He believed that God healed his arm. He told me and my brother that God answered his prayers.

After what happened to my dad, I decided to go to church with my brother and my dad. I wanted to find out about this Jesus for myself.

My brother's friend Steve started talking to me about Jesus. He asked me if I was to die today, would I go to heaven or hell?

I told him I would probably go to hell! I knew that I was a sinner. He then showed me in the Bible in John 3:16 where it says, "For God so loved the world that He gave His only begotten Son, that whosoever believe in Him should not perish but would have everlasting life."

He said that Jesus went to the cross to die for my sins. He told me that I would be saved if I confessed my sins and received Jesus as my Lord and Savior. He showed me in the book of Revelations where it says whosoever was not found written in the Lambs book of Life was cast into the lake of fire. I then asked Jesus Christ to come into my heart and save me. That's how I got my name in the book of Revelations 20. My name was recorded in the book of life.

When I asked Jesus to come into my heart and save me, I was born again. A couple of weeks went by, and I was in my room by myself one night. I was reading my Bible. I was praying to God. I asked God if He would somehow talk to me. He didn't talk to me out loud.

I was reading about Moses. He was standing by a burning bush, and God spoke to him. In that moment, I felt like I was standing next to God. I felt like He was telling me to take off my shoes and that I was standing on holy ground. I did what I felt God was telling me to do. I put my face on the ground, and I started to cry.

That's the day I felt the power of God. It was so real, and God did speak to me. He was speaking to me, and it was so powerful. I couldn't believe it! The power of God was so thick in that room that I couldn't move for at least an hour. I couldn't move, and I was on the ground as if I was a dead man. It was pretty unbelievable, I can tell you that. I started my relationship with God. I had one foot in the burning bush and the other foot still in the world.

CHAPTER 25

Church on Sunday

MY BROTHER, DON, AND I would go to church on Sunday. But on Saturday, we were out partying. It didn't matter if we were at a house party, a beach party, or if we were dancing at one of the local nightclubs.

One Saturday night, my brother and I went down to Redondo Beach where this was this little dance place where all the kids would go to hang out. All you really needed was a fake ID. The bouncers at the door didn't really check out the IDs as closely as they should have. It seemed like all the pretty girls got a free pass to get in. It was called Under the Pier.

It was basically a bar and a dance place. My brother and I were always some of the best dancers. We were always the life of the party. It did not matter where we were, if there was a dance floor, my brother and I were cutting up the dance floor.

I was dancing my heart off when I happened to look up and noticed this Mexican girl. She walked in the room like she owned it. I thought she was the most beautiful girl that I had ever seen. She had beautiful long jet-black hair that hung all the way down her back. She was just beautiful!

I knew in that very second that I was in love. I went right up to her and grabbed her by her hand. I then took her out on the dance floor. We danced all night long, and the rest is history. I guess you could say it was love at first sight.

CHAPTER 26

Turning Point

AFTER MY PERSONAL EXPERIENCES WITH God, God had me meet my wife, Yolanda. That's how much God loved me. She is the only person on the planet for me. God knew what He was doing by bringing her into my life. I felt like there was something different about her. I found out that she was not at all like all of the others girls I had dated. She was so special. The more I was around her, the more I fell in love with her. I wanted to be with her for the rest of my life. We have been together for over forty-five years. This was definitely a God thing.

Meeting my wife, Yolanda, was a turning point in my life. I think God put something special in both of our hearts and minds for each other. Trying to tell you everything that had happened to me before I met her is really hard. My life was filled with sadness and confusion. I did not know what love was.

My life, up until I met my wife, was just about surviving, not caring about myself or anyone else for that matter. I went from not caring about myself or anyone else to caring deeply for my wife and my family. I did not know that it was possible to actually care for someone else's well-being and to love someone more than words can ever express.

I think the reason I love my wife so much was because she was the first one that had ever showed me true love. I would literally lay down my life for her. In the Bible, this is what Jesus did for us.

He laid down His life for our sins. The reason why He did this was because He loved us.

I never knew what love was until Jesus changed my heart. God not only sent His Son to die on the cross for our sins, He gave me a new heart—a heart filled with love and joy. Once I had received Jesus Christ as my Lord and Savior, He gave me my heart's desire which was my wife, Yolanda. Before I met her, my heart was empty, and now I can honestly say that my heart is full.

Sometimes when it comes to my wife, I think I love her too much, but then I realize I just love her the way the Bible tells me to. The Bible says that men are to love their wives as Christ loves the church. Jesus Christ loved us so much that He died for us. True love comes from God. It is a free gift. My life changed after I received Jesus as my Lord and Savior.

Meeting my wife was God's greatest gift to me. My life has been the very best life that anyone could have ever asked for. After I had met Jesus Christ, God gave me my wife. Now the best part of my life begins. I would really love for you to give Jesus Christ the opportunity to change your life the way that He did for me. When you read of all the things that I went through, all the horrible things that people go through, believe me when I tell you that God can change your life. You can have a life filled with peace and happiness. A life filled with purpose.

I felt it was really necessary for me to write my story, *Every Scar Tells a Story*. First and foremost, to give God the glory for changing my life. Secondly, for you to read my story and give Jesus a real chance in life.

I don't believe that a person's life starts until they actually ask Jesus Christ to come into their life. Jesus helped me find my life, and I believe He can help you find your life as well. I will be sharing some of my success stories that occurred after I gave God the opportunity to change my heart. He gave me a new life by giving me my heart's desire.

CHAPTER 27

My Heart's Desire

YOLANDA AND I HAD BEEN dating for a couple of years throughout all our ups and downs, like losing my dad as he died in 1974. After his death, I really went through some tough times. I had a really hard time coming to grips with his death.

I remember one night being so depressed that I put my dad's dog in his 1964 Thunderbird and then drove my dad's Thunderbird into the gate of the Gardena Cemetery where my dad was buried. I'm lucky I didn't die that night.

I drove the car into the cemetery going a hundred miles an hour. I totaled my dad's 64 Thunderbird. It flipped at least three or four times before it came to a stop. If it wasn't for my wife, I don't know what I would've done. She has always been there for me.

We decided to finally get married, and we wanted to start a family of our own together. So in December 1976, we went to Las Vegas to get married. We had a few friends and family members that joined us as we got married.

My crazy friends decided to take the limo that we had rented for a joyride. Never a dull moment with my friends, not even at my wedding.

My brother, Don, was my best man, and my sister, Kathy, was the maid of honor. It was the greatest thing that I had ever done, by marrying my wife, Yolanda. My wife and I took our wedding vows before God and our family and friends very seriously. The love we had for each other was real. God gave us both our hearts' desire. We were now married and ready to start our new life together. With Jesus on our side, we were off to a great start.

Jack and Yolanda Hawley

Jack and Yolanda Hawley

My Wedding Day - Sister Kathy, Wife Yolanda, Jack, Brother Don - 1976

CHAPTER 28

God as Our Foundation

I RECEIVED SOME MONEY FROM my grandma and grandpa on my dad's side, and my wife and I bought our first house in Gardena. We tore it down and made it into a three-unit apartment building. This is where we raised our children, Jack and Angeline. We started going to church together as a family.

Every Sunday morning and every Sunday night, you could find the Hawley family at church. We opened up our home every Wednesday night for Bible study. This really became the strength for our family. Our success story began by making Jesus first in our lives, building our house on the foundation of God.

The Bible says that when difficult times come, and they will, if your house is not built on the solid rock, "which is Jesus Christ," then your house will fall and be destroyed. Your house must be built on the foundation of Jesus Christ. Then, and only then, will your house and your belongings still be standing. It will not be washed away by the waves of destruction. If your house is built on the foundation of Jesus Christ, it will stand the test of time.

This is why I am sharing my true story. Making Jesus first in my life has given me the opportunity to live a life full of God's promises. God has opened doors for me and my family that only He could have. I am so blessed that I did not have to take this journey of life by myself. I have had Jesus by my side every step of the way. He is truly the foundation of our home. You do not have to try to do this thing called life by yourself. Jesus is waiting to help you just as He had helped me. I would like to share how you too could have your home built on the solid rock.

Before I get started, I would like to share a few stories on how God changed my life. I'm going to show you going forward how God works.

One day, my wife and I were praying. We asked God to help us. We needed to hear from Him. We asked God to give us a sign. I remember that night my wife and I went to bed hoping that we would hear from God.

At three o'clock in the morning, my wife and I were awaken to the loudest noise ever. In fact our whole neighborhood was awaken by the loud noise. My wife and I went outside along with some of our neighbors to find out what was making all the noise. We saw that our boat that was parked on the side of our house, the engine had started up all by itself.

At first, I thought that maybe my brother was playing a trick on me by starting the boat because he was always playing tricks on me or trying to scare me. I went outside, and I looked underneath the cover of the boat. I noticed that there were no keys in the boat. The boat could not start without the keys. My wife and I began to get really freaked out as we couldn't believe what was going on.

Then my wife said to me, "Jack, we have been praying for God to give us a sign. Maybe this is the Lord giving us that sign we have been praying for."

We realized at that moment how special God is. That He would start up our boat just to let us know that He hears our prayers. I believe God works in mysterious ways. He has been working and showing me miracle after miracle for over the past forty years. This was just one of the first signs God gave me. This was the start of our relationship with the Lord. Jesus is our foundation, and He wants to be yours too.

CHAPTER 29

Racing Career

AFTER THE CONSTRUCTION OF OUR triplex was finished, we sold it to make some extra money. One of my heart's desire was to race. I wanted to be a race car driver just like my dad. My dad would never allow me or my brother to race while he was alive as he knew how dangerous racing could be.

Coming from a racing family, racing was in my blood. I bought my first race car, a midget, in 1979. My dad was a three-time national motorcycle champion, and he also raced sprint cars and midgets. I always wanted to race. Like I said, racing was in my blood. I had a chance to buy myself a race car as I had some extra money after I sold our triplex, so I bought myself my first midget. It was so much fun.

My first year, I won Rookie of the Year. My second year of racing, I won my first main event. I started driving sprint cars. I got a ride driving for someone else for the very first time, which meant I didn't have to spend any more of my own money on a race car.

When I started racing, I wanted to make sure that everyone knew that I was a Christian. I paid for an ad on one of the billboards at Ascot Park race track. It cost me $5,000 a year; however, I would have paid four times that much if I had to pay for my own race car. The sign reads, "Jesus is Lord." It was kind of funny as they put my "Jesus is Lord" billboard right next to the Budweiser sign.

My billboard was the most talked about thing at Ascot Park. Everyone hated the sign, and they hated me. The races were a place where people would go to watch the race cars. Some of the people went just to see the crashes, but most of the people went to the races to drink and have a good time. And having a sign that talked about Jesus rubbed a lot of people the wrong way. I'm sure that it was confusing to a lot of people.

I was, what you would call, a baby Christian. I would be talking about Jesus one day, and the next day, I would be getting in a fight with someone in the pits. I would fight anyone that looked at me weird. I was a Christian trying to do right. Sometimes I would do right, then again sometimes, I would do wrong.

Regarding drinking alcohol and drugs, this is one of those nights that I did something wrong. I had stopped drinking and doing drugs completely, but then one night, I went down to the beach. I was working on my race car with my mechanic, and some of the guys from my pit crew and all the guys were drinking and doing drugs.

I kept walking by the cold ice chest filled with beer. Looking at all those nice cold beers, I thought to myself, *Oh well, I'll just have one.*

See that's how the devil works. He tells you, you can have one. What is it going to hurt? He's a liar. If you listen to him, he will destroy you. That's what happened that night. I started off telling myself that I would only have one beer. That one beer turned into twenty, and the next thing I knew, I wanted to do a line of coke. Thank God, one of my buddies knew that I was trying to walk with the Lord told me to get out of the room, that I wasn't going to do drugs that night.

I walked out the back door of the house. Right when I shut the door, I happened to look up, and when I did, I saw Mike's cousin who was sitting on the edge of the second floor. Right before my eyes, he slipped and fell backward. As soon as he hit the ground, he was dead! His head split open like a watermelon. I could not believe my eyes. I think I went into shock. I will never forget what happened that night.

Seeing someone die right in front of you will change your life. The police came after talking to everyone, and they had us leave before the coroner got there. I remember feeling so bad for Mike's cousin. He had to be in his early twenties.

I went home and cried out to God. I prayed and asked God to please forgive me. I stayed in and prayed for a couple of hours. God revealed to me that Satan himself wanted me that night. God told me that He told Satan that He couldn't have me, that I was His child because I had received Jesus as my Lord and Savior.

When God revealed to me that Satan wanted my life that night, I asked God to please forgive me. That was the last time that I ever touched alcohol or drugs. I realized that I liked alcohol way too much. I was one of those people that could not just have one drink. I had to stop drinking completely. I will always be the sinner saved by grace. I have learned over the years that as a Christian, it is my responsibility to make the right choices.

My third year in racing, I had the chance to run sprint cars. I won about seven trophies in sprint cars. It was a lot of fun! It is always fun when you win. Everyone is your friend when you're in the winning circle. Like I said, racing was in my blood. Win or lose, I wanted to be at the race track. I wanted the opportunity to run the very best race cars. I knew if I had a good race car, I could run with the best of them.

On the other side of the spectrum, racing was really dangerous. I could have lost my life a couple of times. One night at the races, I crashed really bad. My car was so hooked up and so fast that as I was coming out of turn one and two, my left front tire hit the guy in front of me. I took off like a jet! My car flipped probably three or four times, and when I finally came to a stop, my car burst into a flames. By the time the rescue team got to me, my right leg was burnt pretty bad. I was taken to the hospital where they had to take skin grafts from my upper thigh to repair the burn on my leg. I was in the hospital for six weeks.

It took about eight months for my thigh and leg to heal. Once again, God was watching over me. Accidents are just part of racing. Many of my race car friends have lost their life to racing. I have to believe that God is not yet done with me. He has always kept me safe. Racing will always be in my blood.

I've had the opportunity to race in the Chili Bowl a couple times in my sixties. The Chili Bowl is one of the largest midget events held every year in Oklahoma and has been held for thirty-two years. I could have had the opportunity to race in the Indy 500 if I could have gotten a sponsor for $1,000,000.

Tony George, who was the owner of the Indy 500, told me that I could drive one of his cars if I had a one-million-dollar sponsorship.

One year at the Long Beach Grand Prix, my brother and I decided to go and watch the race. I put on my racing uniform and walked in to the Grand Prix. My brother and I did not pay to get in as everyone assumed I was a race car driver for the Grand Prix. I actually talked to Dale Coin, he owned three Indy cars. And he told me the same thing that Tony George had told me that if I could put a one-million-dollar sponsorship together, I could race one of his cars in the Indy 500.

Billboard at Ascot Park, Gardena, CA

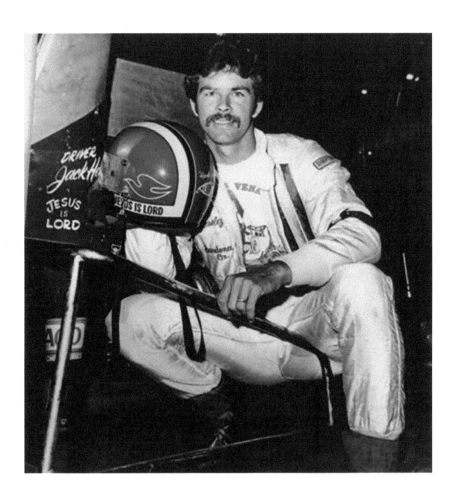

Chile Bowl 2018

Daughter Angeline – Chile Bowl 2018

CHAPTER 30

Carson to El Segundo

WE EVENTUALLY MOVED INTO A condo in Carson. My wife and I were driving our children back and forth from Carson to Bellflower just so our children could go to a Christian school. We did this for about three years. After three years of driving back and forth, my wife and I decided to enroll our children into the public school right across the street from our condo. This was probably one of my biggest regrets.

My son was seven years old and in the third grade when he got in a fight with some boy in his new school. My son, Jack, beat the boy up pretty good. Soon after, the boy's cousin pulled a knife on my son. He told my son that if he hit his cousin again, he was going to stab him.

I went to the school principal. I told him that my son had a knife pulled on him. The boy that pulled the knife on my son was expelled from school. My wife was glad that the boy that pulled the knife on our son was expelled, but she couldn't help but be worried about our children's safety.

One day after school, my son invited a couple of his friends from his class over to our house, and my wife noticed that one of the boys had a tattoo on his hand. He was only seven years old and only in the third grade. My wife asked him if his mom knew that he had a tattoo. He told her that yes she knew and that it was his older brother that gave him the tattoo.

My wife and I decided that it was time for us to move out of Carson, especially after our sons experience with having a knife pulled on him. My wife said that, that was enough, and she wanted out. She was afraid that something bad was going to happen to our children.

We moved to El Segundo, California. El Segundo was a perfect place to raise a family. It was a little town. It reminded me of a little "Mayberry" type town. It was by the beach right next to El Porto and Manhattan Beach. During this particular summer, it had a little shuttle that would pick up the kids from the neighborhood and drop them off at the beach.

Our children loved living in El Segundo. Everything was in walking distance for our children like the schools, the parks, and our church was only a couple of miles from our home. We were going to church.

I'm loving the Lord Jesus Christ with all my heart, and life was great. Our children were doing well in school, and they had made a lot of really good friends. My wife and I decided to purchase our second house. It was right in the middle of the elementary school and high school. Our children went to El Segundo elementary school, El Segundo junior high school, and they both later graduated from El Segundo high school.

Our son, Jack, excelled in both football and baseball, and our daughter, Angeline, excelled in softball. Our son played four years in varsity in both football and baseball, and our daughter played four years varsity in softball. They were both offered scholarships.

It was a real blessing for the Hawley's as my wife and I could not afford an extra $50,000 a year to send our children to a four-year college. We were praying and asking God to please help us, and He did.

CHAPTER 31

San Diego State

OUR SON, JACK, IN HIS senior year, had thirty different schools offer him scholarships in both baseball and football. Jack took the scholarship from San Diego State where he was the starting quarterback for two years. Jack took the scholarship to San Diego State so that his family could watched him play football. It was only a two-hour drive to Qualcomm Stadium, which we made every weekend to watch our son play football.

He was really learning how to play football at the next level. He had to learn the system at San Diego State. His first year at San Diego State, he was trying to understand a prostyle offense compared to a running shoe offense, where he was running around using his athleticism and making plays. To a prostyle offense of staying in the pocket, play action pass was not his strength at all. He had come from Los Angeles Harbor College, which was a junior college in Wilmington, California, where he had broken just about every record that there was. And he was the number one JC recruit in the country.

We were really hoping that his coach was going to put him in the shotgun formation instead of a prostyle offense, but that's not the way it worked out. Jack's second year in the third game of the season, he ended up breaking his neck. He went in and hit the safety instead of going out of bounds. He went back in and collected the safety, and he made the touchdown. But it was a mistake on Jack's part as when he did this, he cracked one of his vertebrae in his neck that put him out for the rest of the season.

San Diego State really helped Jack learn the prostyle offense. In the football community, they really started talking Jack up. Jack had a strong arm coupled with his athletic ability. This made him a perfect fit for a pro team in the NFL. At the end of the season, there were a couple of teams that called him. They were interested in him, but he did not have his doctor's release to let him play yet.

CHAPTER 32

NFL

ON DRAFT DAY, THE RAIDERS wanted to signed Jack. Without his release, they could not sign him. Jack was devastated! He didn't think he would ever play football again. We ended up moving to Cranberry, Pennsylvania.

Because of my thriving cell site business, my wife and I were able to buy a ranch-style home located on fifty-five acres of property. I own my business and was making $205,000 per year, which allowed my wife and I to purchase our home. Not too bad for someone who had only finished the fifth grade. I wish I could take all the credit for my success, but it was all God. God has always blessed me and my family.

One day as I was walking around our property in Pennsylvania, God spoke to me in a way only He could. He told me to put a football field on our property. He told me that my son was going to play football again and that it was not over for Jack. I told Jack what God had told me, and I asked him to pray and ask God to help him. He started working out again. He started throwing the football around on the field of our property.

A month later, Jack got a call from the Buffalo Bills. They asked him to come into their facility. They wanted to give him a workout. He had just gotten his release from his doctor telling him that he had a clean bill of health. My son and I headed out to Rochester, New York, for his workout.

His workout was absolutely perfect. I don't think one ball ever hit the ground. That day, they asked us to stay over. And the next day, they called Jack to come into their office where Jack signed his first pro football contract with the Buffalo Bills. He was on his way, and this was a dream come true for our whole family. Jack went into camp and started working out for a starting position with the Buffalo Bills.

My wife and I took our motorhome to New York to watch our son workout in camp. It was one of the coolest experiences I've ever had. My wife and I were so proud of our son, watching our son participating in the Buffalo Bills facility.

The last day of camp, the Buffalo Bills ended up signing another quarterback. Because of his experience and the fact that the offensive coach had actually worked with him before, the Buffalo Bills wanted to release Jack but then sign him back to the practice squad. However, that did not work out very well for Jack as he got really upset when they released him. If he would have humbled himself and kept his mouth shut, he would have been placed on the practice squad.

Needless to say, he's a lot like me, and he told the coaches how he felt, which didn't help him out at all. What Jack didn't know was that they were going to turn around and sign him and bring him back in. He was young and very immature, and I'm sure he was upset because he felt he worked his butt off. But at the end of the day, he should have kept his mouth shut, but because he didn't, he ruffled some feathers, and they didn't bring him back.

Jack then went ahead and signed with a Canadian team called the Toronto Argonauts. It was three hours from Pennsylvania to Canada, and Jack was just glad he had the opportunity to play football. The fact that he got paid for doing something he loved just made it sweeter.

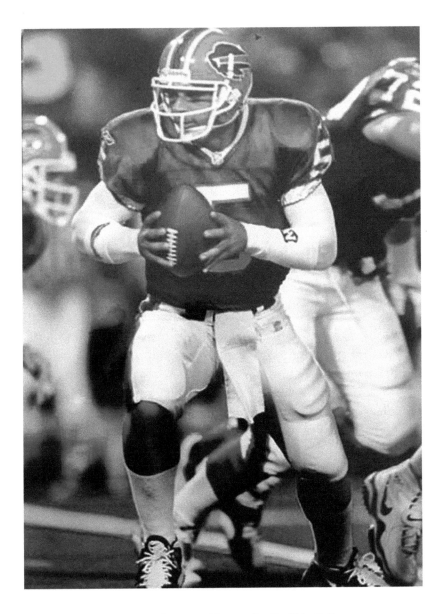

Jack Hawley, Jr. - Playing for Buffalo Bills

CHAPTER 33

San Francisco 49ers

WHEN JACK STARTED SAN DIEGO State, he met this girl who was working at Hooters Restaurant. And within a few months of dating, she became pregnant. And at the age of twenty-one, he became a father.

Jack's firstborn son, Jack III, was born in 2000. He was our first grandson. He was, and still is, the love of our lives. Jack and Jessica were like oil and water. They would fight and make up just to fight and make up again. This went on for years.

Jack and Jessica decided to move to Pennsylvania with me and my wife. And our first grandson was two years old when Jessica and Jack decided to get married. She got pregnant right away, and in 2003, we had our second grandson, Jordan.

They were struggling. They tried, but it just did not work. They were like oil and water. And so in 2009, Jack and Jessica finally divorced. Jack got full custody of both his sons.

My wife and I helped Jack raise both his sons, and when Jack was released from the Toronto Argonauts, my wife and I decided to move back to California. We bought a house in Murrieta, California.

Jack could not get a job with another team as he had to stay in California because of his children and could not leave the state. Jack was still trying to get a job playing football, and he had to play in California. I told Jack that he just had to pray. He had to ask God to give him a team in California. I asked him if he would go with me down to San Diego. I felt it in my spirit that I wanted to walk around Qualcomm Stadium three times—in the name of the Father, Son, and Holy Spirit.

He said, "Dad, you know I love you, but I don't want to go to San Diego and walk around Qualcomm Stadium three times."

I said, "Okay, son, I'm going to go down there for you. I am going to do this."

I felt that I was being asked by God to do this. And so with my faith in Jesus Christ, I went down to San Diego. It was a two-hour drive from my home in Murrieta. I parked in the Qualcomm parking lot, and I was the only car in the parking lot at that time. I started walking around the stadium. In the name of the Father, Son, and the Holy Spirit, I walked around the Qualcomm Stadium three times. And when I was finished, I got in my car, and I started driving home.

I called my son, Jack, and told him, "Son, you are going to get a call to play football, so get ready."

Two days went by, and then on the third day, the San Francisco 49ers called Jack to come in for a workout. Jack couldn't believe it. Once again, God answered our prayers. Jack got his stuff together and went to San Francisco where they signed him. He was going to be playing for the San Francisco 49ers as one of their quarterbacks. He was in the National Football League again.

One day, there was a knock on the door about a week after camp. There were two NFL police officers asking for Jack. Jack was not home at the time. The two NFL police officers told us to get in contact with our son. He had two hours to get to the house. They said in Jack's contract that he was subjected to three random drug tests that he was required to take before the season started.

I called Jack and told him to come home and that he had only two hours to get to the house, that there were two NFL police officers waiting at our house to give him a drug test. Jack came home, and he took the test.

I could tell he didn't want to take the test, but he did anyway. Right before the start of the season, Jack got a call from the head coach of the San Francisco 49ers. He told Jack that they were releasing him because he had tested positive for marijuana. The head coach said he was sorry he had to let him go, but a quarterback for the San Francisco 49ers could not be doing any kind of drugs whatsoever.

We were all heartbroken, and Jack could not believe that he just lost his second chance at playing football in the NFL.

The Bible says your sins will find you out. God is an awesome God. He provided every opportunity for Jack to play football in the NFL. God blessed Jack athletically. He gave him the opportunity to play for the Buffalo Bills and the San Francisco 49ers. Jack was good enough to be one of the best quarterbacks in the National Football League. God wanted to bless Jack, but sometimes because of his sin, he could not. This was in 2004 when marijuana was illegal. Now in California, smoking pot is legal… Go figure.

CHAPTER 34

Work-Related Blessings

I HAVE HAD MANY BLESSINGS in conjunction with my work. Here are just a few of how the Lord has blessed me and my family.

When I lived in El Segundo, my wife and I bought a fifty-six-acre farm in Carson, California. This piece of property came with the entitlements to build fifty-six single family houses. The overhead for this piece of property was thirty-six thousand a month for one year. I got an eight-million-dollar line of credit from the bank. But after I started the demolition and the grading on the project, something happened to the interest rates with the economy, and the banks went completely crazy with all of the interest rates going sky high. The bank that had held the letter of intent to give us our loan for our project canceled the loan, and we ended up losing the project.

In 1999, I started working in the telecommunications industry. I remember being in Richmond, Virginia, in a hotel. I only had $200 in my pocket. I needed a miracle. I was on my knees asking God to help me find a partner. I needed a financial partner to help me start up my new company, building towers for cell phones.

The very first company I went to, Chewing and Wilmer Electricians, gave me a 50 percent partnership and a three-million-dollar credit line. During one of our best years with Chewing and Wilmer, we actually made $600,000 for the telecommunications industry. This partnership lasted eight years. After that relationship, we moved back to California.

I was praying to God and asking God to let me have a large project. I was asking for a hundred-million-dollar project.

After a couple of months, I received the opportunity to be a part of a hundred-million dollar project. I received a line of credit from the company Mastec, whose corporate offices were located in Florida. The project was called the "light squared project."

Parsons, who had the project, gave me the opportunity to do all of the work on the West Coast. I was so excited, but after we started the project, the government stepped in and mentioned some concerns they had about the antennas that we were installing. They were made by a company in Korea, and the government found out something having to do with the antennas that could be a danger to the United States.

They stopped the project, but the bottom line is that God had answered my prayer and gave me hundred-million-dollar project. My wife and I have owned over one hundred pieces of property. These were blessings straight from God. God has always blessed me and my family, and we have never gone without. The Bible says in Matthew 6:33 (KJV), "But seek ye first the kingdom of God and his righteousness; and all these things shall be added unto you."

CHAPTER 35

Grandchildren

ONE OF MY GREATEST JOYS in life has been having the opportunity to help raise my two oldest grandsons, Jack and Jordan. My wife and I wanted to make sure that our grandchildren had the right foundation in life. We believe with all our hearts that Jesus Christ is the right foundation.

We have been able to provide the funds needed to help Jack and Jordan go to a Christian school. They both started Calvary Chapel at the age of four, and our oldest grandson, Jack III, just graduated from a Christian high school in 2018. He is now working at Calvary Chapel.

Our daughter, Angeline, is also working at Calvary Chapel, and her son, Rocky, is now attending Calvary Chapel Christian School.

Every Wednesday at Calvary Chapel Christian School, they have chapel for all children and their families. My wife and I started going to chapel when our oldest grandson was four. This was in 2004, it is now 2018, and my wife and I are still going to chapel, this time to watch our beautiful five-year-old grandson, Rocky.

My wife and I are very proud of the fact that we have been able to help with their tuition. It is truly the best thing we have ever done. God is a God of second chances. One of my biggest regrets was taking my own children out of Christian school, but my God gave me a second chance to get it right.

He allowed me the opportunity to help make sure that my grandsons had the right foundation by sending them to Christian school. I owe my life to my Lord and Savior Jesus Christ. Because of Him, I have been blessed abundantly. My wife and I have been married for forty-five years, and we are still going strong. And it's all because we have built our love on the foundation of our Lord and Savior Jesus Christ. To God be the glory.

CHAPTER 36

My Wife's Blessing

IN 2009, MY WIFE WROTE a book for my two grandsons, Jack and Jordan. Our oldest grandson, Jack, was nine at the time, and Jordan was six. My wife decided to put her story, *Pablo the Bull*, into a little book as an Easter gift for Jack and Jordan.

Once I saw the book and read the story, I told my wife that I was going to have her book published. She just looked at me with her big brown eyes and said that no one is going to publish her story. But I made her a promise that one day I would get her book published for her. And I'm proud to say that today, my wife's first book, *Pablo the Bull*, is being published by Covenant Books and will be available in Barnes and Noble, Amazon, and many other retailers.

Her book, *Pablo the Bull*, will be available in December 2018, along with her second book, *Rocky the Rocket*. My wife had her first book signing at Barnes & Noble in Temecula, California on February 23, 2019. This was just one more of God's blessings.

If you are reading this book, then this is actually my wife's third book that she has had published. Praise be to God. I want to say the best thing that ever happened to me was receiving the Lord Jesus Christ as my Lord and personal savior. The second best thing that ever happened to me was marrying my wife. We both really enjoy going to church and reading our Bible. God has blessed us so much.

The Bible says when we draw close to God, He will draw close to you. Writing this book for you to read is my way of giving back to God for all He has done in my life. If you give Jesus Christ the opportunity, He will bless your life as well.

The Bible says we need to asked Jesus to forgive us for our sins. Believe that He died on the cross for our sins and on the third day, He rose from the grave. The Bible says that we shall be saved. I believe writing this book will help someone receive Jesus as their Lord and Savior and that you will be touched by the Holy Spirit of God. If you will give the Lord Jesus Christ a chance, He will change your life.

God created the heavens and the earth in six days. On the seventh day, He rested. God only wants to bless your life, so please give God a chance to give you a blessing. He is waiting for us to talk to Him, to have a relationship with Him. We can be loved by God. God loves us so much that He gave us His son, Jesus Christ, to die on the cross so that we could have an opportunity to have a relationship with Him. How special is that!

CHAPTER 37

Family Reunion

IN AUGUST 2018, MY WIFE had her family reunion in Madera, California. My wife comes from a very large family. There had to be over two hundred people at her family reunion. I have always wanted to share the Gospel with her family.

I asked her cousin Margie, who had put the family reunion together, if I could share the love of Jesus Christ to her whole family. I wanted the opportunity to get on the platform. For some reason, the family reunion was held at the VFW hall instead of being held outside in a park, and I felt that this was a perfect opportunity to share the love of Jesus Christ.

My wife and I have been married for forty-three years, and her family has had over a dozen family reunions, and I did not want one more family reunion to go by without me sharing the Gospel to my wife's family members.

I shared Revelations 20:15 which states, "Whosoever's name was not found written in the book of life was cast into the lake of fire." I told them how to get their name in that book of life.

In the Bible in John 3, it tells us that we must be born again to enter God's kingdom. I shared that if you repent of your sins and believe in your heart that Jesus died on the cross for our sins and confess with your mouth that Jesus Christ is Lord, that you shall be saved. You could've heard a pin drop from the front all the way to the back. I then led everyone in the room to repeat after me the sinner's prayer. It felt like everyone in the room said the sinner's prayer. It was so awesome! It was an answer to a prayer.

My wife's whole family received Jesus as their Lord and Savior. It was such a blessing for me and my wife, and it had to be one of the greatest moments in my life.

Jack, Jr. and Sairy Hawley 2017

Daughter Angeline and Grandson Rocky 2018

CHAPTER 38

Salvation in Jesus

IN CONCLUSION, I WANT TO finish where I started. If you remember in the beginning of this book, I stated that the reason I was born was to write this book to give hope to the hopeless. The Lord Jesus gives hope to the hopeless. I want you to know that Jesus Christ is the living hope. God has a heart for the hopeless. God is a God of compassion. He will never fail you.

If you're reading this book and you feel hopeless, lost, and all alone, I'm here to tell you that I know exactly how you feel. For you see, I have been in your shoes. I have walked in your pain. I know what it feels like to be hopeless. I know what it is like to want to be loved. I'm here to tell you that today, all that can change because God is love, and He loves you.

I'm going to share some Bible verses with you that will give you hope. After that, I would like to invite you to receive Jesus as your Lord and Savior. The first Bible verse I want to share with you is Romans 3:23 which says, "All have sinned and fall short of the glory of God." Romans 6:23 says, "For the wages of sin is death but the gift of God is eternal life in Christ Jesus our Lord." John 3:16–17 states, "For God so loved the world that He gave His one and only son, that who ever believes in Him should not perish but have ever lasting life, for God did not send His son into the world to condemn the world but to save the world through Him [Jesus]." Romans 10:9 promises that, "If you confess with your mouth Jesus as Lord and believe in your heart that God raised Him from the dead you will be saved."

One of the first things we must do is admit that we have sinned. Then we must repent! The word *repenting* means turning from your ways to God's way. *Repentance* is the decision to turn away from sin and turn to God and obey Him. God wants you to confess your sins to Him. He wants to forgive you.

Revelations 20:15 says, "Whosoever was not found written in the book of life was cast into the lake of fire." You can get your name written in the book of life by receiving Jesus Christ as your Lord and Savior. Remember, it is recorded once you receive Jesus as your Savior.

In John 3:5 (KJV), Jesus answered: "Verily, verily I say onto thee except a man be born of water and of the Spirit he cannot enter the kingdom of God." In Romans 10:13, it says, "For whosoever shall call upon the name of the Lord shall be saved."

If you are ready to receive Jesus as your Lord and Savior, then repeat after me, "Dear Heavenly Father, I come to you with all of my heart realizing I am a sinner. I repent of my sins and confess with my mouth that Jesus Christ is the son of God. He died on the cross for me and my sins. I believe that you raised Him from the dead. Lord Jesus, come into my heart and live in me now. I received by faith, You as my personal Lord Jesus. I know that my name is now written in the book of life. Thank You for giving me hope! Thank You also for hearing my prayers and loving me unconditionally. Please give me the strength, wisdom, and determination to walk in Your will in Jesus's name."

I would like to end this book by thanking my Lord and Savior Jesus for healing all my scars of hopelessness. The scars on Jesus's side, hands, and feet which He took upon himself on the cross were for me. Every scar tells a story... Jesus's scars tells the story of salvation. The end.

Grandson Jack Hawley 2017

Grandson Jordan Hawley 2017

Grandson Joseph

About the Author

YOLANDA JOANNE HAWLEY WAS BORN in Madera, California. She has been married to her husband, Jack William Hawley for over forty-two years. They have two children, a son named Jack William Hawley, Jr. and a daughter named Angeline Sunshine Hawley Walker. She has six beautiful grandsons. The oldest is Jack, age nineteen; Junah, seventeen; Jordan, sixteen; Tony, eleven; Rocky, six; and Joseph, four. She comes from a very large family.

Yolanda has always loved telling stories. As a little girl she would make up stories about her family. Once she got a little older, she would make up stories about her friends. She has always loved making up stories and sharing them with her children, grandchildren, nephews, and nieces. *Pablo the Bull* was her first children's story published in 2018. Her second and third children's books, *Rocky the Rocket* and *Mrs. Roberts & Rascal the Raccoon* will be published in 2019.

Every Scar Tells a Story is a true story based on her husband Jack Hawley.

Yolanda feels she has been very blessed to be married to her wonderful husband Jack, who has encouraged her to use her gift of storytelling to follow her dreams and share her stories. She thanks God every day for blessing her with a loving husband, family, and many wonderful friends. She feels very blessed and says she owes everything to her Heavenly Father.

To: Dave

Thank you for always providing great safety equipment, a win with Simpson, let's win a championship in 2020.

Go Team Simpson!!

Your friend Jack & Yolanda Hawley

Phil 1:6

CPSIA information can be obtained
at www.ICGtesting.com
Printed in the USA
JSHW021404051219
2803JS00003B/15